A Caring Errand—

A Handbook for
Educators,
Future Educators,
and Students'
Caregivers

DR. DONALD J. YOKITIS

PAGE PUBLISHING, INC.
Conneaut Lake, PA

First originally published by Page Publishing 2021

ISBN 978-1-6624-2420-5 (pbk)
ISBN 978-1-6624-2421-2 (digital)

Printed in the United States of America

CONTENTS

PREFACE

THIS BOOK IS intended, first and foremost, for elementary teachers, secondary teachers, for those who guide the learning of students with special needs, and school administrators. Principals may well want to utilize this book during teacher in-service days at both the elementary and secondary levels. Small groups of educators could cooperatively summarize the materials and plan how they may use the suggestions in their instruction. Other populations who may well profit by reading this book are parents, university-education majors, and professors of education. Everything said in the upcoming thoughts apply equally well to the instruction and encouragement provided by caregivers to their children and youth via home schooling or by way of virtual learning. The professors could utilize the book to supplement their courses' textbooks.

The forthcoming thoughts and reflections are the fruits of over fifty years of scholarship and over fifty years of teaching and tutoring. The work reflects an underlying commitment to students and families.

Care has the final say in this effort to promote the interests of all students. Caring binds together children and their significant adults. Caring is the dynamic that makes the world of students and adults go around.

INTRODUCTION

THIS SHORT BOOK paints pictures of effective classroom management, elementary, secondary, special-education-instruction, and moral-education. The discourse is about the interaction of teachers and students that brings about the growth of both. Both the theory and practice of education emerge from this concise statement. Three theories of education underpin the practices involved in schooling.

When elementary and secondary practices are under discussion, core subjects are highlighted. At the elementary level, the focal points are on reading, math, language arts, science, geography, and health and physical education. At the secondary stratum, the focus is on English, science, social studies, reading in content areas, health and physical education, and students' quest for self and moral maturity. All the disciplines exist within the framework of behavioral-management practices.

There are three theoretical perspectives that foster learning. They are thinking theory, interactionalist theory, and the philosophy of caring.

First, thinking theory can be understood as being analogous to the workings of a computer. In both cases, information is taken in, processed, and acquired by either the mind or by the computer's processing system.

Second, interactionalist theory is learning that has been socially acquired. It is realized in interactions with—students' peers and with more learned adults.

Third, caring is, without a doubt, the bedrock of all learning. It is the motivating force that underpins both cognitive and social learning.

CHAPTER 1

Caring

CARING IS THE characteristic most sought after by students. It is the foundation upon which all learning occurs in classrooms. The art of teaching is based on caring and additionally calls out for the creativity of teachers. The science of teaching encompasses the technical skills of teachers and their application.

Caring teachers find joy in all aspects of teaching: planning, instructing, guiding learning, and evaluating. These teachers do not find their work cumbersome; they are so in the flow of the classroom process that they are scarcely aware of themselves as doers. Such teachers effortlessly apply the art and science of teaching. They elevate interest and kindness to art forms. By modeling these two ideals and by encouraging children and youth, these instructors involve students in course content, kindness toward others, patience, and universal respect. These four virtues can be fleshed out by way of examples.

First, interest is something that emerges from the presence of a person or object. Caring teachers evoke attention by their personal presence and by the manner in which they provide instruction and guidance of learning. For example, a student who evidences no interest in academics was drawn out when involved in spelling unfamiliar words. The initial concern led to a level of interest in other academic subjects.

Second, kindness is fundamentally a spiritual virtue. Kindness is benevolence, which can be engendered in children and youth through its practice by teachers, and permeates all aspects of classroom practice. For example, interest in course content and all class members is a natural consequence of benevolence or kindness.

Third, patience is understanding, which evidences generosity of thinking, feeling, and acting toward others. For example, a youngster struggling to decode words in the context of stories is advantaged by the patient support of the reading teacher.

Fourth, respect is, first and foremost, a calling to sustain interest, provoke kindness, and enliven patience. For example, a student suffering from social and emotional disabilities learns to practice respect when unfailingly treated with value by all class members.

Classroom learning occurs most effectively when students experience success by helpful thoughts, feelings, and actions of their teachers and by an atmosphere marked by interest, kindness, patience, and respect. The art of teaching ends up being more important than the science of teaching. Instruction flows from the art of teaching with its four defining characteristics. Teachers and students are carried along in the flow of academic, social, and personal achievement when caring and its concomitant virtues are extant.

CHAPTER 2

Behavior Management of Students in Their Schools and Homes

INTRODUCTION

EFFECTIVE CLASSROOM MANAGEMENT is the point upon which all other aspects of schooling pivots. Skillful classroom management is the building constructed through healthy teacher-student relationships and by teachers' creating warm, cooperative, and generous classroom environments that motivate students to meet the requirements of the curricular goals.

Classy Classrooms

Classy classrooms are ones in which warm rapport exists. The rooms are characterized by the leadership of teachers and initiative on the part of the students. A graceful flow and academic achievement are present.

The boundless energy of the youngsters is harnessed by the teachers, who utilize the vigor of the atmosphere. Once harnessed, energy is released in productive work. Teachers lead the youngsters to successfully master the curriculum.

Gracefulness among class members is the hallmark of a constructive and joyful classrooms. As needed, teachers model what is expected and, through instruction and guidance, permit students to pursue goals of choice and to select from a menu of objectives to accomplish.

In well-managed classrooms, less is more. Teachers seldom find it necessary to intervene. Teachers and students pull in the same direction. Lack of stress allows students to flourish academically and socially. Success for all is a reality, not a pipe dream.

Three School and Classroom Management Measures

Students burdened with psychological, emotional, or learning disabilities or encumbered with the need to inappropriately seek attention often face negative sanctions at school. The formal consequences are time-out, suspension, and expulsion from school. The three behavior-management measures have proven effective in bringing negative behavior of students in line with school and classroom expectations.

First, persistent disruptive behaviors or consistent failure to complete assignments often result in time-outs. The length of exclusion is normally for one day. Students receive counseling while in a time-out room and then return to class.

Second, suspension is a more restrictive placement option. It is assigned when students fight or engage in unabated disruptions of school or classrooms. Suspension is typically from three to ten days. Counseling and teachers caregivers conferences take place before excluded students may return to school.

Third, expulsion for a calendar year is the most restrictive of the three corrective strategies. Assault, distribution or use of controlled substances, and possession of weapons warrant expulsion and, in many cases, criminal charges. Satisfactory completion of homebound instruction and counseling are required before pupils may return to school.

The three behavior management measures are, most often, effective in curtailing antisocial behaviors of students. Effective counseling and out-of-class instruction are the keys to transitioning students from exclusion to fully included members of school and classroom communities.

The Traits of Effective Classroom Managers

In schools, classroom management involves supervising a group of students. Among the traits of an effective manager are understanding, poise, integrity, vigilance, warmth, and the ability to structure a happy and productive environment. Teachers model what is allowed and disallowed in the classroom.

Skilled teachers build classroom climate. Positive climates and positive selfconcepts thrive in environments of caring, cooperation, warmth, and everpresent helping hands.

Expert instructors know not to act negatively nor to think and speak negatively to their pupils. Thoughts are communicated without speech. Negative thoughts break down trust, self-esteem, and the ability to perform. Ostracized students do not fully benefit from classrooms of academic-centered activities.

A specific and long-standing classroom management strategy has three steps when violations occurs. First, the transgressors are reminded of the rules. Second, natural consequences are assigned. Finally, violators are invited to fully participate in the flow of classrooms focused on learning that makes inappropriate behaviors unlikely.

Classroom supervision is about poise, understanding, integrity, vigilance, warmth, and the construction of joyful and productive classrooms. Students benefit from such positive classroom management.

Classroom Management and Student Growth

Growth is fundamental to the health and well-being of children and youth. Academic, social, psychological, and spiritual development by way of a structured and academically centered classroom occurs when students and teachers work alongside one another. Ideally, all class members are carried along in a stream of mutual support and cooperation. Collaboration supersedes competition as the dominant classroom strategy. In competition, there are winners and those who lose out. In cooperation, everyone is a winner.

A multicultural approach is the one that encourages growth. The increase in diversity of American society cries out to all segments of the nation to become more inclusive. The variety of cultural, social, ethnic, economic, language, and educational elements are promoted by open-minded teachers and students alike.

In caring, structured, and tolerant classrooms led by open-minded teachers, everyone finds a home. In such settings, teachers practicing leadership principles encourage appropriate and productive work. In all of this, respect and concern for others' rights are ever present. Students grow in such environments.

Classroom Management and Students' Self-Regulation

Classroom management is the process by which behaviors are shaped, allowing youngsters to self-regulate. Teachers structure environments in order that students may achieve goals. Effective flow or cooperation happens when classroom management is present.

Teachers' modus operandi is central to success. Teachers lead the way by modeling and productive conduct. Instructors strive to build positive classroom climates and to ensure the development of positive self-concepts. These environments are beacons of warmth, structure, and the presence of helping hands.

Dos and don'ts are important for teachers to model self-discipline and have students practice self-regulation. Overarching objectives of modeling and helping students are necessary to realize self-discipline. Rapport that is ever present enables students to enjoy joyful and productive classroom climates.

Teachers Hold Much of the Power in the Classroom

Teachers are the most powerful member of the classroom. Some of the power is, however, given up to students as they advance through the grades. Youngsters become empowered when they increasingly take charge of their learning. Selfmotivation, self-discipline, high expectations, and energy are empowerment's components.

First, students are enabled when they are self-movers. To foster independence, teachers do not do anything for students that they can do for themselves. At the same time, when insurmountable barriers surface, youngsters are assured that the teacher's helping hand is present. Self-moving is the right mix of students' independence and the presence of more expert adults.

Second, self-discipline is vital to learning. Empowered students may be temporarily sidetracked while reading or listening to lecture. The key to restoration of focus is reflection. Youngsters return to the task at hand when they realize their minds have gone elsewhere.

Third, high hopes empower students. Low expectations weaken pupils. Learners who expect high-level performance achieve at high levels.

Fourth, vitality empowers students. Vigor fuels self-motivation, self-discipline, and high expectations. Attainment of worthwhile purposes occurs when students are empowered, invigorated, and when power is shared.

Classroom Management: Teachers' Most Difficult Challenge

Alienated and indifferent students present teachers with their most difficult challenge. These youngsters have been victimized by unhealthy environments and genes. Among the impairments are psychological, social, intellectual, and academic deficits. Many are at risk for school failure and are students with special needs.

The path to well-being is one of cooperation. An individualized education program is a core intervention.

Along the way of the specially designed plan, students gradually grow in selfconfidence and resiliency. As youngsters learn to risk failure and find success enable, they blossom.

The role of teachers in creating classroom climate is crucial to the accomplishments experienced by students. The record of teachers is exemplary in elevating the performance of the formally alienated and indifferent students to successful ventures.

Classroom Management: Student Growth and Classroom Flexibility

During the process of growth, a turning inward and a turning outward occur. The inward push is a matter of marshalling positive thoughts and emotions. The outward pull happens when intentions and actions are congruent. In both actions, resiliency or flexibility of thinking is central. Resiliency, along with the two actions, is apparent in students. Resilient and properly motivated youngsters achieve at high levels academically and socially.

In classrooms where flexibility flourishes, students feel free to take risks. Such freedom is vital for significant achievements.

For considerable development in schools to transpire, appropriate objectives must be designed. Teachers are mindful not to set goals too high or too low. Goals that are too high frustrate students; too low goals stifle achievement. A happy medium is called for. Under such circumstances, youngsters grow.

Power of Positive Incentives

The lure of good grades is powerful. As are valued by students and families. Students who earn the awards for academic excellence realize personal goals and have elevated self-esteem. However, some youngsters fail to earn the treasures and suffer low self-esteem. Among these students are those who underachieve. Schools and teachers make heroic efforts to elevate the performance of youngsters who struggle in school for three reasons: unhealthy home and neighborhood environment, a mismatch between instructional materials and students' learning levels, and a discrepancy between teachers' strategies and students' learning styles. These three disabling conditions are subject to corrective measures.

First, unhealthy home and neighborhood environments are not within purview of schools and teachers. Nevertheless, teachers can style environments that are healthy and provide an oasis for learning.

Second, the incongruency between instructional materials and the academic levels of students is readily fixed. During teacher in service days, materials can be gathered that align with students' instructional levels.

Third, in-service time can be utilized to design tactics that match students' learning styles. Hope abounds when instructional materials and teaching techniques align with students' needs.

High grades provide powerful incentives for students. However, for students who underachieve, good grades earned by peers are reminders of failure. Nevertheless, through teachers' efforts, droves of previously minimally-successful students are experiencing success.

Three Ways of Knowing are Present in Classrooms

Present in classrooms are intuitive learning, learning from direct instruction, and cooperative learning. The three processes are centered on imparting and receiving information and gaining knowledge from teachers' instruction.

The first way of gaining knowledge is intuition. Intuitive knowledge is an immediate grasp of a fact or sentiment.

The workings of direct instruction and group learning often give rise to intuitive insights. For example, a student may unlock the secrets of solving a word problem or the means of setting a purpose for reading without teachers' interventions. The contents of mathematic and reading classes are invaluable in fostering the children's achievements. As a result, these students gain skills in mathematics and reading classes.

The second technique is direct instruction. In this teacher-centered strategy, youngsters capture understandings and learn skills. The knowledge and abilities gleaned enable students to better achieve knowledge intuitively.

The third tactic is cooperative learning. In this practice, teachers assign tasks for collaborative groups and roles for each participant. The students then work to complete the assignment with little teacher intervention. After the chores are completed, each group presents its findings.

The three methods yield learning gains. They occur naturally in classrooms and benefit all learners. The skill and vigilance of teachers maximize benefits.

Productive and Healthy Classroom Management Notions

Stylish, productive, and healthy classrooms are characterized by positive management, appropriate reinforcement, and a flow of mutual strengthening. Corrective and progressive supervisory programs help both students who are struggling and those who are flourishing.

Children who strain both socially and academically endure negative consequences; those who blossom rarely face such measures.

In a system of effective school and classroom supervision, more attention is given to those who experience difficulties. At the same time, care is given to those who benefit most. The idea is to nudge those who are underachieving into the flow of classroom productivity and inclusion while keeping those who are performing well in the same stream.

For students with special needs, pupils who are underachieving, and those who are at risk for school failure, an individualized education program is advised. The regimen has three steps: First, current academic and social levels are assessed. Second, measurable objectives are developed. Finally, on the basis of assessments, diagnostic-centered instruction is set into motion.

School and classroom management systems, along with an individualized programs, most often work miracles. Students benefit from the well-structured and student-centered systems. For this to happen, schools and classrooms need to set limits in which style and productivity rule.

Compassionate and Wise Classroom Management

In the thoughtful, warm, and structured classroom, teachers take the first step in avoiding punishing students who do not benefit from strict discipline. The second step involves the judgement and the skill of teachers in substituting fair classroom management for a propensity to punish.

Behaviorally impaired youngsters are typically chastised at home, in the neighborhood, and at school. They suffer emotional, psychological, social, and learning deficiencies. Most often these students are from families living in impoverished neighborhoods. They are students with special needs, those who are underachieving, or pupils at risk for school failure. These heavily burdened youngsters act out to gain attention they are not receiving elsewhere. Their behaviors bring on penalties. Already under duress, the negative consequences add to the discomfort of the learners.

To rein in the anxiety and aberrant behaviors, teachers may exercise judgement and compassion by applying reasonable and fair limits to the behaviors in question. Youngsters who struggle to self-regulate welcome boundaries. They come to embrace the fundamental class rule: act so as to allow all class members the opportunity to enjoy an orderly, inviting, and productive environments.

It cannot be stressed too strongly the need for success that all students possess. Students need to consistently experience academic and social accomplishments. Well-conceived management plans all but guarantee the success of each and every class member.

Classroom Management: Preventing Unnecessary Punishment

Through structure and compassion, classroom teachers can avoid punishing students who do not benefit from negative sanctions. Intelligent and sympathetic application of reasonable consequences are legitimate routes to appropriate discipline. Rules set the limits, and when violations occur, natural consequences are applied. Teachers are mindful of the intolerable conditions under which many repeated offenders live. These students are heavily burdened with social, emotional, and psychological disabilities. These same children land in trouble at school. They are punished at home, in neighborhoods, and in schools.

Teachers' caring and structured classrooms can make a difference. Professionals who set reasonable expectations for each child arm learners with the skills and knowledge to meet the requirements of curricular goals. Objectives need to be neither too high nor too low. Unreasonably high goals frustrate children. Too low expectations block learning. A happy medium alone enables children to flourish.

SUMMARY

Effective classroom management was discussed in terms of teachers encouraging pupils, including students with special needs, to make uncommon efforts to accomplish objectives set forth by the schools' curriculum and goals of personal choice. Almost without exception, general-education and special-education teachers generously implement the instructional and assessment requirements that foster meaningful achievement of the schools' most vulnerable youngsters. Ideally, students are self-starters and motivated finishers. In reality, few students are so activated. Because of this, teachers deliberately and creatively design and implement sensitive and logical reinforcement regimens to supplement what students bring to the table. Importantly, passionate and competent instructors support students' efforts to succeed by building and maintaining friendly relationships among all class members and by creating caring, structured, and productive classroom environments.

CHAPTER 3

Elementary and Secondary Education

INTRODUCTION

THIS CHAPTER PROVIDES facts about what actually occurs and what ideally happens in elementary and secondary classrooms. A number of examples serve to bring alive the discussions. All elementary and secondary subjects are presented. In addition, the power of warm teacher-student rapport and of cooperative and productive classroom climate are highlighted. In addition, without a doubt, the most important elementary, middle school secondary school subject, as well as special education subject, is reading. The BDA system, along with its easy to use chart, is an effective means to enable both children and youth to effectively comprehend factual and fictional texts.

Children Requiring Reading Instruction

Worldwide, millions of children enter kindergarten ill-prepared to read. These youngsters are usually from impoverished homes. They have not benefited from the enrichment that leads students to reading readiness. These children are in a race that they are not aware of. If they are not at grade equivalency by the end of third grade, these children are fated to fall further behind.

Hope, however, abounds for these ill-prepared children. Teachers and specialists are mindful of early interventions starting at the preschool level. Concerted efforts need to be made beyond the school house; caregivers need to contribute. Typically, a folder travels between school and home. Books and worksheets are intended to reinforce and enrich what is being taught and practiced in school.

In school, specially designed reading programs are planned and delivered from preschool through third grade as needed. Additionally, high school and university recruits may support teachers by providing one-on-one instruction.

Reading comprehension at the third-grade level can be improved by structuring the reading process. The three stages of the reading process can be taught and practiced until mastery is achieved. The method involves interconnective steps detailing what to do before reading, during reading, and after reading.

When reading practice and reinforcement are part of the daily round, children succeed. Students grow in the ability to decode words and read for comprehension. These children are winning the race.

Overcoming Reading Disadvantages of Children

It is not an exaggeration to say that school success or failure begins in the womb. Preschool and primary school education are vital to ameliorate the powerful negative impact of heredity and language-poor homes on children. The prospects of children thus handicapped is poor in the absence of early intervention. The keys to effective remediation are a structured and caring classroom environment, a warm and success-oriented teacher, and one-on-one instruction.

First, the classroom needs to be orderly and distress-free; the learning climate is child-centered. Reading well is the top priority. Teachers are vigilant in calling on children and keeping their minds focused on phonic lessons and on comprehension of stories of various genre.

Second, competent and caring teachers employ sound reading tactics. They have the children repeat mispronounced words and have them search out answers to questions on workbook pages.

Third, for youngsters reading below grade equivalent, one-on-one tutoring is typically provided. When children are grouped by reading level, the one-on-one is made available by classroom aids, by university students, and by adult volunteers.

Success or failure in reading begins in the womb. However, being disadvantaged is not destiny. Productive classroom environments, effective teaching, and one on-one tutoring are paving the way to competency in reading by droves of children.

Elementary Reading Instruction

Elementary teachers are working intelligently and constructively to help children master the complex skills that make up the reading process. Four competencies constitute the process: decoding, vocabulary, oral reading, and silent reading.

First, decoding is stressed in the primary grades and entails building words from letters. Teachers use their reading manuals, smart boards, children's workbooks, and storybooks to teach phonetic rules and to provide students practice in decoding. Young readers are asked to read words in sentences projected onto smart boards found on workbook pages and embedded in stories. Repetitive reading, until 100 percent accuracy is achieved, is a powerful tool in enhancing children's word-attack skills.

Second, vocabulary acquisition is made possible by students' abilities to build words from letters. The store of words that arises from drill on word lists and through the repeated reading of stories is substantial. One widely used tactic utilized by teachers is pausing the reading and then asking children to define target terms in their own words. Teachers then make corrections and guide students to more accurately describe the vocabulary words.

Third, oral reading provides children with a crucial means of practicing decoding, reviewing familiar words, and learning new terms. Additionally, oral reading promotes fluency and fosters reading comprehension. Repetitive oral reading, until 100 percent accuracy is realized, ensures that young readers make meaningful gains in reading proficiency.

Fourth, silent reading foreshadows and prepares children for successful reading at the secondary level and beyond. In this reading strategy, youngsters read their assigned storybooks and are also free to choose books within the ranges of their reading aptitude. After reading a book, the children are asked to formulate reports by listing book titles and its author and by writing brief summaries of the books' contents. The narratives are invaluable to teachers as comprehension checks and in supplying youthful readers with positive reinforcement. The narratives work miracles in encouraging children to read more outside the classroom.

Reading at the elementary-school stage has decoding, vocabulary, oral reading, and silent reading components. Through the elementary teachers' planning and application of sound tactics, children are enabled to realize meaningful accomplishments in reading's overarching goal of comprehension of fictional and nonfictional texts.

Reading Is a Thinking and Socially Realized Activity

Reading is a thinking activity that is socially realized; meaning is built in this activity. The theory and practice of reading includes fluency, expressiveness, and comprehension of varied texts.

For children, it is crucial that their teachers amply supply time for oral reading. All three competencies are best developed and evaluated through oral reading. Fluency leads to expressiveness and expressiveness to comprehension.

As children read, teachers provide comprehension checks by asking questions that beg factual and inferential responses. The responses connect stories being read with other stories and to experiences outside of school.

A number of contextual elements are germane to understanding stories: main idea, cause and effect, sequencing, and comparing and contrasting are some of the elements. Workbook pages, library books, and weekly readers provide the means for teachers' evaluation of knowledge and skills.

Finally, it is crucial to reading success at the elementary level that stories and workbook pages are reinforced in the children's homes. Children need to read to caregivers on a nightly basis.

Reading is a thinking activity. The affirmative process occurs in the students' minds. The social aspect involves interactions among the children, their peers, teachers, and caregivers. The best efforts of all who are involved typically help to develop the three elements of reading.

Teaching Science in Elementary Schools

Creative, organized, and energetic science teachers fully engage their students in experiments and in cataloguing activities. Three examples illustrate what takes place in the best science classes.

First, experiments are central to the daily hands-on science round. Greater learning occurs when textbook and Internet information are utilized. For example, the law of gravity is best taught and learned through an unforgettable experiment. In the demonstration, students take turns dropping objects and come to realize that an unknown force must be propelling the object downward. By reading their science textbook and online information, pupils come to know that the force is gravity.

Second, an experiment gives a clear sense of how science study proceeds in a student-centered and dynamic classroom. The impact of hot and cold on metals is made real through a hands-on experiment. When a metal rod is heated, it easily slips through a metal hoop; when the same rod is cooled, it cannot pass through the same hoop.

Third, a classifying exercise rounds out the three thought-provoking investigations. The study of animals is one of many cataloguing inquires carried out in the course of the school year. Five species of the animal kingdom are studied and classified. They are mammals, amphibians, reptiles, fish, and birds. Then cats, dogs, lions, and racoons are identified as belonging to the mammal species.

Experimental learning and learning through demonstration and classifying are the pivots upon which active science learning revolve. Science teachers preplan hands-on learning lessons, enabling students to fully enjoy and benefit from a yearlong science adventure.

Health and Physical in Elementary Schools

Health and physical education classes are integral to schools' efforts to foster physical, psychology, and educational growth of children. The twofold venture is a cooperative effort by students and teachers. Health and physical education classes provide for physical exercise and set forth guidelines on healthy eating practices. Along with supplying intense exercise and dietary guidance, health and physical education teachers provide opportunities for students to finetune basic and gross motor skills. The former proficiencies can and are nurtured through games such as darts and making notes while reading health textbooks and internet sources. A large array of games serves to develop gross motor skills including basketball, baseball, softball, roller-blade hockey, and soccer; they foster learning to compete with rivals and cooperate with teammates. In addition, these games tend to stimulate the growth of endurance, flexibility, and strength.

The psychological aspects of children are also addressed through competitive games and instruction about competing as good sports. The heat of contentious activities provides for stress release in the short term and builds resiliency in the long term. The stress relief garnered through participation in competitive games builds the ability to cope with future challenges. Direct instruction and the study of health-related vignettes work miracles in self-understanding and in the ability to successfully cope with life's challenges.

The health and physical education classes provide for educational games in relevant knowledge and capabilities. Skills such as reading with comprehension and successfully writing essays and reports are honed. The mathematical proficiencies of interpreting and constructing graphs and charts find a home in health classes.

Health and physical education are important elements of schools' curricula. Physical, psychological, and educational components of students' growth are provided for in health and gym classes. Health and physical education teachers are the touchstone in enabling students to attain and maintain healthy lifestyles and physical fitness.

Teaching Mathematics in the Elementary School

Successful elementary math teachers utilize manipulatives, direct instruction, games, smart boards, and seatwork in instruction. The start-off point is the instructional level of the class, which is determined by diagnostic testing, teachers' observations, and early-stage work samples.

Effective use of manipulatives precedes and lays the foundation for the mastery of math facts, computing proficiency, and the efficient solving of story problems. Counters or other manipulatives are employed to enable children to realize competency in the three areas of elementary mathematics.

Direct instruction reinforces what has been realized through hands-on learning. The value of focus teaching cannot be overstated. Expert math teachers deftly guide learners to understand and apply basic arithmetic facts and computation skills to real-life problems.

Games strengthen what has been achieved through hands-on learning and by direct instruction. Games that provide drill on basic math facts, computation practice, and story problems extend students' knowledge and skills.

The final teaching tactic is the efficient use of smart boards and seatwork. Specifically, children work the same problems at their desks as classmates work at the board. Teachers make corrections as needed.

Teaching math in the elementary school focuses on the use of manipulatives, direct instruction, learning games, the use of smart boards, and seatwork. Students prosper when a variety of instructional strategies are put into practice. Success for all math pupils is thus made likely.

Hands-On Activities Form the Core of Math, Reading, and Geography Instruction

In the core elementary subjects, hands-on activities play a pivotal role in transforming abstract concepts into lively realities. Initially, reading and math are largely hands-on subjects. In math, counters are used to make concrete abstract numbers. For example, the number 5 is paired with five counters. In reading, single letters are cut out and matched with words. For example, the letters *d*, *o*, and *g* are overlaid on the printed word *dog*. Such practices lay the foundation of all learning that follows in reading and math.

Perhaps no larger part is played by hands-on learning than in geography. The course is manipulatively based, spatially oriented, and successful in transmuting geography's abstractions into concrete truths. The curriculum usually starts with the identification and location of large landmasses and large bodies of water portrayed on wall maps. Cut-outs of the oceans and continents are compared to what a large wall map depicts. Once the children are able to name the largest physical features on earth, they take turns in cooperatively assembling the cutouts on magnetized smart boards. The final task for the young children is a daunting one. They are asked to list on paper and cooperatively assemble on the whiteboard the names of the five oceans and seven continents.

The value of this physically based process spills over into all areas of the elementary curriculum. Importantly, the stress-relieving process frees youngsters to more fully engage with the school's two-core subject of reading and math.

Elementary Teachers Interpersonal Skills Are Invaluable

Elementary teachers are responsible for teaching the important subjects of reading, math, and language arts. In addition to instructional skills and content knowledge, the teachers' interpersonal capabilities are invaluable in guiding children to meaningful achievements in the three essential subjects.

Interpersonally, the instructors are both taskmasters and nurturing. They take charge during instructional blocks while being especially caring during seatwork and at recess.

Through the expert utilization of learning games, teachers witness to their interpersonal and instructional knowledge and gifts. When games are employed, elementary teachers focus their attention and those of their pupils on educational content germane to reading, math, and language arts. For example, a teacher may design a math game in which primary school children are called upon to answer addition and subtraction facts presented on flash cards. Two teams compete in the activity with the winning group earning tokens used to purchase learning materials or toys.

Another game involves providing a basketball hoop and nerf ball. In this competitive contest, students earn a point by correctly naming sight words or accurately spelling words from their weekly spelling lists. An additional point is earned by making a basket. Players on the winning team become eligible to fill classroom-helper rolls such as line leader and the job of passing out and collecting materials.

Elementary school teachers are responsible for teaching reading, math, and language arts. Task-focused yet nurturing teachers make likely meaningful achievement by their pupils in the three basic subjects.

Recess

Recess is more than an add-on to the primary elementary school education. It is an essential part. The minimally structured sessions contribute to students' proficiency in reading, writing, and math in three ways.

First, recess enhances concentration and endurance. After the release of excess energy, students can more carefully attend to their school tasks. Also, physical activity leads to increased hardiness, enabling the children to persist in working the roughout the day.

Second, social skills are built during recess and spill over into periods dedicated to academics. Indoor and outdoor recess allow for friendly competition. Most often the games involve only the children. At times, teachers contend with the youngsters. When indoors, a variety of learning goals may be addressed in fun ways. For example, sight words and addition facts can be learned and reviewed through games.

Third, school enjoyment is heightened through daily recess. After the break, children more easily make progress in the three Rs. Moreover, attendance improves; children want to be in school. Reading, writing, and arithmetic form the core of elementary school education. Recess supports and fortifies all three. Release of nervous energy during recess leads to greater academic and social output. Children are freed to be fun-loving and are reenergized to attend to the curriculum's more intensive work.

Elementary and Secondary Reading Instruction

Learning to read high school textbooks, journal articles, and internet materials require the best effort of students and teachers alike. The before, during, and after reading process is the vehicle that carries learners to significant gains in reading comprehension and skills. The procedure is underpinned by two theories: thinking scheme and a culturally sensitive mindset.

First, thinking scheme may be understood in terms of a metaphor. The computer and the human mind operate similarly. Both receive input from the environment. The mind and the computer then process the information by employing mental or technical processes. Both of them organize, categorize, compare and contrast, and analyze and synthesize information. After receiving and processing the information, the human mind and the computer generated output—that is, knowledge for the mind and data in the case of the computer.

Second, a culturally sensitive mindset centers on a multicultural theme. The theory and practice of a multicultural notion is based on the realization that social interactions are inseparable from learning in general and from learning to read content-area texts well. The students' interactions with peers and with more expert adults allows teenagers to more efficiently unlock meanings hidden in the texts. Three concepts and processes emerge from constructivism and culturally sensitive theories.

To begin with, when students and teachers discourse about the meaning of a segment of course content, they typically arrive at a common understanding. Teachers are not commanding the discussion but are allowing for mutuality. In order to best advantage culturally diverse students, it is a sound practice to guide students along the way of understanding varied texts.

Cooperative learning is an effective means of practicing a tool that brings to life content-area readings. A graphic organizer allows students to track and pace their efforts in reading selections meaningfully. The chart has three columns headed consecutively: before, during, and after. During the early stages of learning, the readers pair up to work on the organizer. The first of the three columns initiates the organized reading of texts. The first phase has students predict what the text will be about after reading its title. Then the pupils further anticipate the text's content by creating two or three questions they want answered by reading (See Appendix A-BDA). During reading, students answer the questions they have created and make notes on the back of their charts (See Appendix B-Notes). Finally, the reading session concludes with the youngster taking a quiz or complete a vocabulary maping exercise (See Appendix C-Vocabulary Mapping) or writing a summary that presents their ideas and other interesting information found in the texts.

Reading is an activity involving thinking scheme, culturally sensitive mindset, and the reading of culturally relevant materials. The entirety of the reading process requires a mastering of content-relevant texts. The teachers' efforts and ingenuity ensure that every student enjoys gains in content-area reading knowledge and skills.

The Importance of Vocabulary in Secondary Reading

Knowledge of vocabulary by students at every grade level is essential to comprehending a vast array of required and freely chosen texts. Reading any selection involves participation in three sequential steps that are before reading, during reading, and after reading.

Before students read a selection, they cooperatively identify important vocabulary words and jointly fashion preliminary definitions. The pupils then use the terms in sentences. The engaging practice involves all students. The social give-and-take heightens individual and group learning.

During reading, vocabulary terms are revisited. A powerful strategy for reinforcing the learning content-specific words involves both teachers and learners. Teachers halt the reading periodically and call on students to answer who, what, where, when, and how questions. Answering the queries brings to the surface meanings of words that were heretofore beneath the surface of consciousness.

The after-reading step affords an important moment for students to deliver vocabulary terms into memory and a final occasion to deepen their comprehension of reading passage. A concluding activity invites pupils to completing graphic organizers encompassing both vocabulary and comprehension elements (Appendix C-Vocabulary Mapping).

In school, vocabulary is mastered individually and cooperatively by students. Key terms in reading selections are collaboratively defined, used in sentences, and cemented into pupils' consciousness during reviews. Most importantly, command of important terms heightens comprehension of reading texts of varied lengths and complexity.

Teaching the Social Sciences at the Secondary Level

Studying the social sciences can be an enjoyable, rewarding, and enlightening experience for both students and teachers. Among the reasons for the positive impact of the study are that it leads to an accumulation of meaningful knowledge, results in a flowering of academic skills, and engenders broadening worldviews of student and teachers amidst a multicultural landscape.

First, through an engaged examination of history, world cultures, and cultural geography, students gain rich storehouses of knowledge. The learning is gleaned through presentations by teachers, cooperative-group participation, and by reading textbooks and internet information.

Second, in addition to reading and writing proficiencies, research skills are vital in achieving the enlightenment, which is the touchstone of the successful study of the social sciences. The research process has seven steps: identifying a problem, gathering relevant information, organizing, analyzing, summarizing the data, testing the hypothesis, and reporting findings.

Third, ever-widening worldviews by both students and teachers is crucial to the social science enterprise. A multicultural mentality directs all class members to recognize and appreciate persons of diverse ethnic, language, racial, learning, social-economic classes, and persons with special needs.

The study of social studies is invaluable to students and teachers alike. The knowledge and skills acquired through the study are invaluable. Perhaps the greatest value that emerges from the adventure is the expanding worldviews of students and those who are privileged to teach one of the school's most important subjects.

Secondary School Mathematics

Mathematics is a core subject at the secondary level. It is driven by the goal that all students gain a command of the important knowledge and skills relevant to solving practical problems and gaining competency with computing. To this end, math teachers guide their pupils toward achieving curriculum goals. Students and teachers forge alliances in accomplishing objectives they share.

Two examples serve to illustrate the process of mathematics instruction and learning. First, higher-level computation skills are presented which take pupils well beyond what they learned at the lower levels. The growth in higher-level thinking and computational skills is typically remarkable for youngsters in grades 7–12.

Second, craftsman-like study in solving word problems with practical applications engender the successful reaching of math standards. Students are given the skills to solve problems they may face in adult life. General math, algebra, geometry, trigonometry, and calculus are the subjects most typically offered. Mastery in these subjects prepares students for success in postsecondary education and, potentially, for math-related careers.

Through adept planning, instructing, assessing, and (when necessary) reteaching, math teachers empower their students. They help them gain success in mastering one of the most challenging and rewarding subjects offered by secondary schools.

Secondary-School Science

Physical science, biology, physics, environmental science, and chemistry are the core science subjects at the secondary level of education. Becoming proficient in any of these disciplines is a collaborative enterprise of teachers and students. Science instructors do their part by performing three instructional duties.

First, science teachers thoroughly plan each lesson. They are ready and able to guide pupils so that they can grasp the complex knowledge and experimental skills germane to scientific principles.

Second, secondary-science teachers center instruction on experimental and cataloguing exercises. For example, in biology, amphibians are studied through lectures, textbooks, and the internet. Also, a dissection of frogs can provide much useful information. Furthermore, laboratory notebooks are utilized so that students can record data. The final step involves writing summaries to determine whether or not key principles have been acquired.

Third, in physics and chemistry classes, many experiments are conducted on a weekly basis. In physics, one topic deals with the impact of heat and cold. In chemistry, the three states of matter are a frequent study.

Secondary sciences compose a rewarding and important discipline. The rewards include the development of inductive and deductive reasoning skills, the building of inquisitive propensities, and the honing of collaborative abilities. The study of the sciences develops a forward-looking perspective that prepares students for success at the college and postcollege level and, for some, science-related careers.

Secondary-School Health and Physical Education

Health and physical education at the secondary education level focuses on convincing students of the advantages of healthy living and being physically fit. Health education classrooms, gymnasiums, and playing fields are the arenas where the development of healthful living and fitness habits occur.

In health, classroom teachers deliver instructions on how to live healthy lives. The curriculum's emphasis is on proper diet, daily exercise, and developing sound social relationships. To this end, maintenance of psychological well-being and the importance of life-sustaining rest are stressed. To achieve these ends, the use of texts, body models, smart boards, internet information, and teacher lectures are heavily utilized.

Gymnasiums and playing fields are employed to heighten students' physical fitness. In these two arenas, pupils' strength, stamina, balance, and agility are enhanced. Games such as flag football, basketball, softball, soccer, volleyball, and long-distance running are among the activities that foster athleticism and fitness. Long-distance running plays a special role by building students' endurance and determination, which holds them in good stead during mentally and emotionally draining school days.

Secondary-school health and physical education attempt to promote healthful living and physical fitness. The courses challenge teachers to plan carefully, instruct thoroughly, and assess accurately.

Through the collaborative effort of both teachers and students, healthy habits are attained and maintained at high levels of proficiency.

Vocational-Technical Education in Secondary Schools

Vocational-technical education is an increasingly important part of secondary school curriculum. Three factors define the burgeoning impact. First, work ethic is learned and practiced during the daily round of schooling that focuses on hands-on careers. Second, resiliency blossoms when obstacles are overcome while students work to complete projects that connect schools with communities. Third, technical skills are cooperatively acquired when youngsters complete tasks that find homes outside of formal school settings.

Work ethic emerges in and is practiced during various undertakings. Future vocational-technical practitioners learn to report to school and worksites on time and to work with energy and determination in completing tasks.

Cooperation is about teaming. Cooperation is found in every vocational-technical area including carpentry, masonry, automobile mechanics, plumbing, building trades, culinary arts, cosmetology, computer programming, and prenursing curriculum. All these skilled crafts provide fertile soil for learning and practicing the art and science of cooperation. For example, work ethic, resiliency, and technical skills come into play during the time building-trade students collaboratively construct storage sheds. The projects are launched when the students gather the materials and tools needed to build the sheds. The work culminates when building-trade classes have delivered sheds to their customers' properties.

Future careers emerge from time well spent in an array of vocational-technical pursuits. Along the way, work ethic, resiliency, cooperation, and technical skills blossom and are practiced. Budding skilled workers partner with and model the work habits and attitudes of their teachers. The students are remarkably successful in the here and now and look forward to bright and prosperous futures in vocational-technical careers.

Student Growth and Multicultural Education at the Secondary Level

Education is about change and growth. The starting point is schooling from kindergarten through twelfth grade. Beyond formal education is a life-long journey of development. The adventure is a multicultural one. The existence of a diverse world impels students to learn about many traditions. One of the cultures to be studied is the American Indian culture.

Through an open-minded appreciation of the American Indian, change and growth occur.

A metaphor enlightens efforts to understand the basics of American Indian traditions. The metaphor is the circle. This allusion speaks to the continuation of life, connectiveness, and shepherding.

Circular arrangement of teepees evidences the lived experience of shared power and solidarity. The life cycle is portrayed as a journey from birth to death.

The study of Native American culture is part of an investigation of multiple traditions. Hundreds of traditions are the subject matter for students. Change and growth occur when such a study is undertaken. As usual, teachers apply leadership principles in leading the way to knowledge.

Two Ways in Which Secondary Students Gain Knowledge

There are two ways of coming to know. Intuition is the first vehicle. Experience, coupled with mental processing, is the second. Schools and teachers are centrally concerned with enabling students to attain knowledge.

Sudden realization occurs in all people. Meditation is a more laborious process that also results in learning.

Empirical-rational knowledge issues forth when the senses encounter the world and when the mind builds meaning from sense data. The scientific method is invaluable in coming to know. This inquiry involves seven steps: identifying a problem, studying the relevant research literature, stating a research problem, formulating a hypothesis, testing a theory, gathering data, and reporting findings.

Schools and teachers can teach and have students practice the ways of gaining knowledge using intuitive-based and empirical-rational techniques, which are central to the education of teenagers. Teachers are widely successful in this endeavor.

Three Kinds of Knowledge Acquired by Secondary Students

The core of education is knowledge. Knowledge is three-fold: objective, subjective, and the knowledge that comes from faith.

Objective certainty has to do with physical reality. Knowledge in this first realm focuses on reading, writing, arithmetic, English, science, social studies, and scientific inquiry. Knowledge is coaxed out of the curriculum through the scientific method. Careful study, formulating hypotheses, and arriving at verifiable conclusions are the basis of the method.

Subjective knowledge lies outside of verifiable knowledge and the scientific method. It involves opinion and what the heart longs for. These understandings lie in the heart and mind of the beholder. The curricular subjects most applicable to subjective truths are literature and philosophy.

Faith-based knowledge is often seen as lying beyond the curriculum. Faith-based knowledge emerges from the study of social sciences, religion, and philosophy. The study of these areas of the curriculum often results in the knowledge that is held passionately and inwardly.

Finally, students should be thankful for the guidance their teachers provided them in acquiring knowledge by both objective subjective means. Understandings realized by faith are the final fruits of these inquiries.

Language Arts at the Elementary and Secondary Levels

During the elementary years language arts curriculum includes: spelling, penmanship, and English. For secondary students the instruction they receive from their teachers centers on literature, creative writing and research—based writing, and for some, the study of a foreign language.

The study of language arts begins in the elementary grades with a focus on penmanship, spelling, grammar, capitalization, punctuation and the writing of paragraphs and stories. These are the basics of instruction and study.

The writing of essays in grades 4–6 typically entails teachers' instructing and modeling a three- step process made up of an introductory paragraph, a three–paragraph body and a concluding paragraph. Through consistent practice and by careful guiding hands of their teachers the children are empowered master simple yet effective writing process.

At the secondary level, the language arts curriculum's focus is on literature, creative and research–based writing. Students are taught how to brainstorm in order to come up with a writing topic, to build an outline, to write a rough draft, to edit their work and to complete their compositions.

A final portion of the language arts package at the secondary level is the study of foreign languages which is valuable in itself as a means of communicating with others. Foreign language study also helps students to better understand effectively utilize their given languages.

The study of language arts at the secondary level culminates, for most students, in a senior project requiting a research paper and presentation. The pupils are challenged to execute an exacting research process. The research begins with the identification of a topic of interest, a statement of a research problem, a thorough study of the scholarly literature germane to the topic under investigation, the gathering of data, the analysis and summation of the information and the reporting of the findings by, most often, a power point presentation.

The study and mastery of language arts at both the elementary and the secondary levels empowers students to comprehend varied texts at high levels of proficiency and to clearly communicate orally and in writing. Through the study of language arts students develop and fine-tune their higher thinking skills such as analyzing, synthesizing and evaluating. The skills serve the youngsters well in their postsecondary and not- too-distance career endeavors.

The Assessment of Elementary and Secondary Students in Education Settings

Ideally, the evaluation of general education students has three phases: pre-instructional, instructional and post-instructional. The three stages will now be discussed in turn.

The pre-instructional phase entails both formal and informal elements. The formal assessment is paper and pencil, computer-based or by means of hands-on activities. In the academic subjects of reading, mathematics, sciences, social sciences, English and literature current functional levels are determined. The hands-on subjects targeted by teachers for assessment are art, music, health, physical education and the vocational-technological education.

During the instructional phase students are again evaluated both formally and informally by their teachers. For example, pupils reading fluency can be formally determined by means the reading a story orally and their reading comprehension assessed by means of a reading comprehension quiz.

Ideally, the assessment of elementary and secondary general education students has both formal and informal aspects. As just discussed the process is made up of three phases: pre-instructional, instructional and post-instructional that not only evaluate how students are currently doing but, more importantly, encouraging, through positive feedback, higher levels of academic and hands-on learning.

SUMMARY

In this chapter, elementary and secondary-education instruction spotlighted the necessity of effectively providing for quality teaching assessment of reading, science, social studies, mathematics, health and physical education, and vocational-technical programming. It is recommended that the BDA reading system be used to instruct, not only secondary students in all content area subjects, but also every elementary and middle school student. It provided information on how teachers enabled students to grow socially, academically, psychologically, and morally. Curriculum objectives were shown to be effectively accomplished through teachers' and students' partnerships.

CHAPTER 4

Special Education

INTRODUCTION

NUMEROUS STUDENTS HAVE been found to be in need of specialized education and instruction and auxiliary accommodations. These are student with special needs. The forthcoming discussion focuses attention on the needs and programming required to address the educational goals of these students.

Traits of Effective Special-Education Teachers

There are at a minimum five traits that distinguish superior special-education teachers from those who are just learning the art and science of teaching students with special needs. The five characteristics are patience, kindness, humor, commitment, and soundness in knowledge and skills.

First, the self-discipline and ethical special education teachers are unfailingly patient. Importantly, forbearance is taught and modeled in special education classrooms and resource rooms. As pupils copy the model of patience, it becomes the defining quality that they embrace. The abstract concept may be fleshed out by way of an example. When youngsters struggle to read a passage, teachers patiently supply the correct words for those that are mispronounced. Special-education teachers then have pupils read the selection until 100 percent mastery has been achieved.

Second, effective special-education teachers are dependently kind and understanding. They witness to the principal that legitimate educational goals do not justify less than kind means. Students with special needs, along with peers without disabilities, respond best and learn more when teachers are both benevolent and tolerant. Pupils bask in the glow of kindness and discernment that emanates from the special-education mentors. For example, special-education teachers need to realize that children will most likely struggle to achieve competency in counting coins and telling time. Success in mastering the two important life skills results from instruction, modeling, and practice time allotted to students with disabilities by their teachers.

Third, the teachers' humor is a hidden motivational force. Humor enlivens classrooms and contributes to positive and warm teacher-student rapport. In turn, the high-quality rapport fosters the academic, social, and vocational prosperity of students. For example, reading fun-filled stories or constructing collages with humorous motifs rejuvenate students to better engage in more demanding academic subjects. Such experiences go to the heart of the humor that forges friendships among all class members.

Fourth, service commitment is central to special education teachers' efforts to have their pupils mount obstacles to achieve important curricular objectives. Resiliency is initially achieved when a challenge is overcome and then flourishes as obstacle after obstacle is conquered. For example, students who failed a science test find the courage to consult with their science teacher in order to jointly plan an intervention. This intervention proceeds sequentially from listening better in class, more fully participating in class, more effectively preparing for tests, and by applying study tips during exams.

Finally, efficacious special education instructors have eminent content-area knowledge and refined instructional skills. The teachers' knowledge and skills are conveyed to their exceptional students and result in high-level knowledge and skills that hold them in good stead while in school and in the world beyond school. For instance, creative and scientific writing courses are essential for school success skills, which are applied in social studies, in the sciences, and in English courses are vital to students' success in their future careers. The same competency is germane to careers such as business, law enforcement, and vocational endeavors.

These five character traits enhance the ability of veteran special-ed teachers to thoroughly mentor at a higher level than is possible for newly certified teachers. Each trait is necessary for special educators to effectively work with their pupils to achieve academically, socially, and to blossom in knowledge and future career endeavors.

Resiliency in Special-Education Instruction

Resiliency is present in every person and in every age. Attention may be focused on the school environment and youngsters. The abilities exhibited by students are focus, determination, and the ability to bounce back from disappointments. Typically, youngsters realize significant and social gains. Three cases will follow.

Through home support and teacher instruction, a child leap-frogged four reading levels during the first quarter of the school year. Her confidence and self-concept blossomed.

The second of these occurrences documents a child's struggle to tell time. The student eventually mastered the understanding and skills necessary to tell time through his own persistence and through his teacher's support.

The final case highlights the efforts of a child to track objects. After many trials, the student experienced success. With the pathway to learning opened, the child was able to achieve important understandings such as recognizing his teacher by the sound of his footsteps.

Students can achieve important school-related objectives with the support and aid of caring, talented, and devoted teachers. It is of the utmost importance that each and every child experiences success. They can realize academic, social, and spiritual growth. Children's lives are changed significantly when they realize fulfillment.

Two Dimensions of Special and General Education

Learning is vital to the well-being and prosperity of students. Education, of which schooling is a part, has both macroscopic and microscopic dimensions. These two parts of education stem from experience.

The first dimension of macroscopic education occurs in general education classrooms and in vocational education. Schooling is conducted by professional educators who use formal and informal assessments on a daily, weekly, and yearly schedule. The information is utilized to adjust objectives and instruction.

The second dimension is the microscopic. Students who are not able to achieve the objectives for their grade level after careful evaluation and general education accommodations are assigned part-time or full-time to special education. In the special-education classroom, youngsters benefit from one-on-one and small-group instruction much more than they can receive in general classes. The overarching goal is to return these children to full-time inclusion with peers in regular-education classes.

The process is not perfect and is subject to adjustment. In fact, teachers focusing on the individual youngster are able to adjust instruction to meet the needs of both the general and special-needs students.

SUMMARY

Students with disabilities have been described in terms of their educational requirements and in terms of the instruction necessary to meet their needs. These pupils have been discussed with a focus on their learning disabilities, intellectual deficits, emotional liabilities, and in some cases, their autistic tendencies. Teachers' efforts to build warm, productive, and cooperative teacher-student rapport and structured classroom environments were stressed.

Teachers were portrayed as caring, self-disciplined, instructionally sound, and unfailingly respectful. Students with special needs were seen as the beneficiaries of their teachers' gifts. The planning, instruction, and assessment provided by individualized educational programs were reported to be the centerpiece of the education of students with disabilities. The programs are legally binding on both special- and general-education teachers.

CHAPTER 5

Moral Education

INTRODUCTION

THIS CHAPTER IS about moral education. When properly planned and modeled in schools and by teachers, children and teenagers blossom in caring and become virtuous family members and fair-minded, responsible citizens inside and outside of schools. While numerous strategies exist for enlightening youngsters in the morals of their culture, modeling is the most powerful. The idea is "to do as I do." The present and future happiness, satisfaction, and productivity of youngsters' lives is critically determined by the quality of their ethical maturity.

Teachers Empower Students to Become Ethically Mature

In the best classrooms, teachers empower their students to become ethically mature. The classroom environment fosters respectful speech, politeness, and helpfulness or service.

First, when respectful speech is effectively modeled by teachers, it is usually emulated by their pupils. They openly and respectfully communicate with classmates and teachers during class discussions, in collaborative learning groups, and by way individual presentations.

Second, politeness is the second virtue found in ethically developing youngsters. Courtesy energizes gift-giving youths and those who receive the gift. Small acts of graciousness transform students and teachers alike. With every gesture of politeness, students and their mentors come closer to achieving the ideal of a polite and harmonious classroom climate.

Third, helpfulness or service becomes real when it is concretely expressed through generous deeds. Holding a door for another or assisting a classmate in solving a stubborn math problem are acts of service that refresh the helper and those who are served. Students who serve are changed each time they assist others. They become willing attendants.

When youngsters are properly supported by their teachers and classroom environments, they invariably discharge their duties of communicating respectfully, interacting politely, and serving where service is needed. These students are on their way to achieving moral maturity.

Duty and Respect—Two Virtues Taught and Modeled in Schools

Duty and respect have been long taught and encouraged in homes, neighborhoods, and schools. When any of these environments fail to adequately teach and model these virtues, one or more of the stalwarts assumes a larger role. In contemporary America, shortcomings in homes and neighborhoods have necessitated schools to make up for their deficiencies. Schools strive to design and maintain environments in which duty and respect may thrive. Meanwhile, teachers redouble their efforts to carry into practice rules that support the widely accepted values.

In practice, the high-minded and desirable principles change the person who carries them out and those who receive the gifts. The first ideal is duty, which is the performance of what is morally obligatory. Second, respect is a discharging what is owed to all others. In both cases, all deeds of mercy, kindness, understanding, and compassion are works of duty and respect.

School and classroom processes are crucial in building the character and moral rectitude of youngsters. Rules, reinforcement, modeling, and the study of morally-laden stories constitute the core of school and classroom ethical education.

Children and adolescents learn the wisdom of accepting the two-honored virtues through the training they receive in schools, neighborhoods, and homes. Students come to know that virtue is its own reward. By acting dutifully and respectfully, they reap personal, social, and ethical fruits.

Respect and Responsibility: Essentials to Teenagers' Moral Maturity

Moral maturity is, in part, a gradual unfolding of the virtues of responsibility and respect. The two ideals are taught and modeled in the home, at work, in the neighborhood, at church, and in school. For example, by completing chores at home, teenagers learn and practice responsibility. Respect is made real by bowing to the authority of employers. Finally, a myriad of school tasks allows students to carry into practice the two moral tenants. For example, a youngster saddled with attention and hyperactive syndrome is advantaged in school by an understanding teacher. The easily distracted student is permitted to work on assignments in the back of the classroom. The teacher's efforts are rewarded when the student completes assignments at a high level of proficiency.

Respect is typically not hard to engender in teenagers. Direct instruction in the ways of properly respecting others and modeling allows adolescents to grasp and practice the virtue. In addition, books and internet vignettes portraying tolerance as an ideal and intolerance as a counter-ideal invite students to respect all persons they encounter.

Responsibility and respect can be and are taught and modeled in one's daily encounters. Full acquisition of the two virtues awaits a student's full maturity. Educators and caregivers who interact properly with teenagers heavily impact the moral growth achieved by them.

Teenagers and Their Ethical Selves

There are a number of contenders for what lies at the core of the self. The candidates are pleasure, power, possessions, and spirit. Pleasure, power, and possessions belong to the body; spirit belongs to the soul. Since the soul is superior to the body, elements associated with the body cannot be the essence of the self. Spirit alone is at the self's core.

Humans by nature are spirit. They naturally care about others. In the case where religious faith is present, humans care about God. The essence of a person is spirit. However, among the throngs that suffer depression or lack of spirit, there is loss of hope. They lack the positive traits of energy, commitment, enthusiasm, and love of others. These youth are trapped within themselves. They need help to escape. Help is available from caregivers and teachers. At the secondary level, cooperation with the home is integrally involved in enlivening adolescents.

A warm and structured classroom, along with compassionate and committed teachers, is the means of allowing the spirit itself to flourish. For the true self to emerge, consistent, effective instruction and modeling are crucial. Largely through the design and careful implementation and through the alliance between home and school, success is realized. Previously despairing teenagers reclaim their spiritual cores.

Teenagers' Search for an Ethical Self

Adolescents are engaged in a search for an authentic and an ethical self in which concerned adults play supportive roles. Teenagers seek to uncover who they are and who they want to become. Along the way, two dimensions of self are unearthed while a third is shrouded in mystery.

The first dimension of self is defined by social roles. Teenagers try on a variety of roles such as musician, athlete, and employee. Internally, the roles throw into disarray the quest for genuineness. Adolescents are more than their roles.

The second dimension of self is that of unique potentiality. Teenagers find a flickering experience of selfhood by projecting toward a not-so-distant future that calls for forward planning and doing.

The third dimension of self is a perplexing one. While the social self resides uncomfortably in the present and the self of possibilities is not yet real, the enigmatic self remains unfulfilled in adolescents. The third dimension of personhood remains but a shadowy entity, which is the object of the teenagers' search. It is their real self.

Interested and active adults are important supports in the adolescents' journey to finding an authentic self. The adults, however, play ambivalent roles. On the one hand, they support teenagers' current roles and future plans. On the other hand, by allowing adolescents appropriate freedom, the more mature allow for a journey to selfhood that is neither integral to teenagers' present state nor to their other future possibilities.

Ethical Virtues Taught at the Secondary Level

Character or virtue education is both implicitly and explicitly taught in schools and classrooms. Courage, determination, fairness, and integrity are modeled and directly taught. Students can understand these ideals by reading morally-laden literature. They can see and feel the virtues in the actions of teachers and classmates. Virtues come alive through course content and modeling.

Courage is the first of the moral virtues. None of the other ideals can be realized without valor. For example, eighth-graders demonstrate courage by befriending a classmate who has been shunned.

Determination is the second ideal. Steadfastness of mind and action is evident when students strive to complete assignments and urge peers to do likewise. For example, the goal of mastering multiplication tables necessitates considerable individual effort. However, cooperative work not only leads to group success but also results in individual accomplishments.

Fairness is the third virtue found in high-minded people. Fairness is treating all others with respect. Fairness can be seen in classrooms and on the playground. For example, while at play, students most often honestly officiate their games.

The final ideal is integrity, which unites the other three virtues. Integrous persons are true to who they are. Persons of high character or virtue are fully integrated. Through school curriculum and modeling, students are well on their way to achieving high character and integration.

Independence, Responsibility, and Productivity: Social Virtues of Adolescents

The powerful agents of socialization do much to determine what occurs in the lives of teenagers. Family, peers, school, mass media, and work significantly shape who adolescents are and will become.

School is particularly important since teenagers spend more of their waking hours in school than in any other setting. Formal training in society's mores, values, and goals occur in classrooms. Importantly, one agent of socialization fades in importance in high school. Peer pressure diminishes in significance as compared to the sway it held previously. More mature adolescents are forward-looking. While taking seriously academic tasks, they view them in terms of future designs. Teenagers take seriously their present and future independence, responsibilities, and productivity.

For adolescents, independence entails freedom from restrictions and freedom to make choices. Significantly, teenagers will sometimes make decisions independently from their parents' wishes. For example, these budding adults make take on part-time jobs.

Responsibility is learned through social interaction. Duties are, in part, acquired in classrooms where students obey rules. Responsible adolescents respect all members in the class and never disrupt the classroom flow.

Productivity is one of the hallmarks of a civilization. Groups cannot survive without the productivity of their members. Teenagers at work are important parts of their societies.

Adolescents are subject to the dynamics of socialization. They respond with resiliency in growing in independence, responsibility, and productivity. Schools and teachers mightily impact that growth.

Global Ethics

Both youngsters and adults know of the benefits enjoyed and scourges suffered by people throughout the world. Due to internet technology, travel, education outside the classroom and schooling such knowledge is unavoidable. All students learn to embrace the understandings.

Even more, droves of students choose to act on budding global awareness. At the urging of their families, schools, and teachers, youngsters are helping the needy at home and in distant lands. They are stuffing boxes with essentials, raising funds to feed the hungry, and promoting global solidarity through adept use of the internet. By and large, students accept the fact that the blessings and needs of the earth are unevenly distributed. People living in postindustrial countries are resource-rich and enjoy comforts; people in the developing world are resource-poor and endure discomfort.

The uneven allocation of the planet's goods motivates youngsters to step up and help those who endure the inequality. These children and youth are serviceoriented. They minister because they are enlightened and large-hearted. Such youngsters do not see national boundaries when ministering to the marginalized; they feel solidarity. These youngsters are their brothers' keepers.

Education in Citizenship—An Important Virtue Taught and Modeled in Schools

Education in citizenship begins in the primary grades and extends through senior high. Communication is one of the building blocks of citizenship. Among the civic enterprises are working for political campaigns, attending political rallies and speaking to peers about local, national, and global concerns.

Schools and teachers are supporting engagements in the problems faced by all of humanity. Among the issues are pollution, hunger, starvation, natural disasters, and low-level voter turnout. A further concern is the shrinking globe. This phenomenon represents a two-edged sword. On the one hand, the mass media has brought people closer together. On the other hand, the discourses are often superficial and impersonal. The internet, cellular phones, television, and compact discs have supplanted face-to-face and intimate letter-to-letter discourse. Political rallies and debates are no longer avenues of genuine discourse; they have become arenas of name-calling, manipulation, and propaganda.

Along with homes and neighborhoods, classrooms afford children and youth the means for authentic and clear communication. Daily verbal and written opportunities provide students with the wherewithal to communicate effectively and engage meaningfully in their communities. Through instruction and practice, youngsters are transformed from uninformed and dispassionate students to informed and passionate citizens.

Elementary and Secondary Art and Music: Two Paths for Integrating the Aesthetic and Ethical in the Lives of Students

At first, glance art and music at the elementary and secondary levels of education appear to be strictly aesthetic endeavors. However, these pursuits are equally ethical in nature. They change the artists and musicians internally and serve to enhance the lives of the peers and adults who see or hear their creative productions.

Art is fundamentally a thinking and feeling activity that is expressed in concrete products. For example, youthful painters and sculptors fashion creations that transform them into more caring and service-oriented individuals as they witness the awe that their outcomes engender in others. Artists and musicians alike are inspired to strive to become their better shelves; those who appreciate art and are similarly emboldened to strive to become their very best selves.

Music, as with art, is at its foundation a thinking and feeling activity that produces melodious compositions. Band and chorus members are transformed by engaging in the process of performing beautiful music; they are elevated spiritually and ethically. At the same time, those who enjoy the music are moved to realize their spiritual and ethical potentials by being more concerns about others.

Elementary and secondary art and music are engagements that transform artists, musicians, and audiences alike. These aesthetic and ethical pursuits bring together all who create or simply appreciate the artistic products and enthralling performances. The vital role of schools and teachers in instructing and guiding the transformative process cannot be overstated.

Moral education and development have been described in terms of virtues. A diminished role was assigned to the impact of principles in the modeling of students' moral attitudes and actions. It was found that caring is the most practical and effective virtue and is what binds respect, honesty, benevolence, and responsibility together. Adolescents were viewed as engaged in a search for self, which turns out to be a quest for moral rectitude. The probe centered on freedom and responsibility or what is necessary for journeys to moral maturity.

CONCLUSION

THIS CONCLUDING CHAPTER has been about moral educa-
tion, which charts out paths to moral maturity. One tried-and-tested
method of instructing youngsters on the road to realizing caring and
virtuous lives is the reading and discussion of texts that teach ethical
lessons.

Perhaps no other virtue is as vital to students' present and future
success as respect. Respect binds together all moral virtues in a manner
that almost inevitably leads youngsters to a quality of life unthinkable
through any other means.

Many other worthwhile means have and are utilized to instruct
and guide children and youth along morally sound avenues. Such roads
offer happiness, fulfillment and success in life.

EPILOGUE

THE CENTERPIECE OF this book is teachers' and caregivers' skillful, structured, and compassionate classroom and home management systems. In addition, the programming necessary to properly instruct students in general and special educational classrooms is stressed. The teachers' and caregivers' creative and diligent work in empowering students to take charge of their own academic, social, vocational, emotional, and moral growth has been stressed. Such development is made likely when students and teachers and caregivers work collaboratively in safe, warm, and organized schools and classrooms and home settings. Caring, an attitude and action, has been portrayed as teachers' and caregivers' unwavering confidence in children and youth. Such certainty enables students to live productively and joyfully in the here and now and in the future.

Care has been presented as the lived dynamic that makes the world of youngsters and involved adults go around. Insights and positive work on the part of adults allow students to achieve success in school and beyond.

APPENDICES

APPENDIX A
BDA

Before	
My Knowledge	My Questions
During	
Answers to Questions	Notes

After

My Choice (Check)

_____ Structured Notes   _____ Research and Present

_____ Written Summary   _____ Concept Mapping

Name- _____   Subject- _____   Strategy (B-D-A)

Date- _____   Pages- _____

APPENDIX B
NOTES

I.
    A.
        1.
            a.
            b.
            c.
        2.
            a.
            b.
            c.
        3.
            a.
            b.
            c.
    B.
        1.
        2.
        3.
    C.
        1.
        2.
        3.
II.
    A.
    B.
    C.
III.
    A.
    B.
    C.

APPENDIX C
VOCABULARY MAPPING

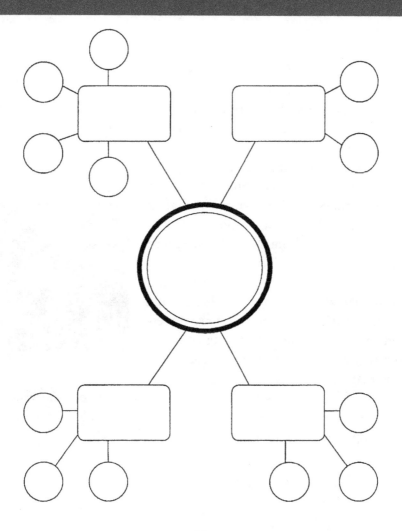

ABOUT THE AUTHOR

DR. YOKITIS HAS been a serious student for over fifty years and a teacher-professor for forty-six years. His formal education includes earning a bachelor's degree in elementary education from Slippery Rock University, a master's degree in special education from Shippensburg University, a social studies certificate from St. Francis University in Pennsylvania, and a doctor of education degree from Nova Southeastern University in Davie, Florida.

Dr. Yokitis taught general education and special education in grades 2–12. On a part-time basis, he has taught at the undergraduate and graduate levels. Finally, Dr. Yokitis continues to tutor high school and elementary-age pupils.

Dr. Yokitis and his wife, Sue, reside in Nanty Glo, Pennsylvania, and are the parents of three adult children: Benjamin, Sarah, and Julia. The couple are the grandparents of Miles and Annabelle.

CPSIA information can be obtained
at www.ICGtesting.com
Printed in the USA
BVHW031143220921
617298BV00005B/62

9 781662 424205